Moon At Midnight

Late night conversations under the moon

Mariela Lazcano

BookLeaf Publishing

India | USA | UK

Made with ❤ on the BookLeaf Publishing Platform
www.bookleafpub.in
www.bookleafpub.com

Dedication

To my Family,
Wether you are the family I was born into or family I made along the way. This step forward is for you. For in my darkest times you were my light. It was you that pulled me out of the deepest depths of mind. Never giving up on me when I had given up on myself. For speaking life back into me when I felt there was nothing left. For giving me a shoulder to cry on and an embrace when needed. I may not always have the right words, but please know without you life would have no color.

All my love forever and always.

Mariela Lazcano

Preface

I always felt like I was broken growing up. I was always sad about something. It frustrated my family. I did not understand of course until the birth of my son. Through watching him grow. I realized I never healed or let any of these things that hurt me go. I bottled it up and pretended it did not exist. That no blood was ever shed.

Instead I would sit outside under the moon these poems are the result of my conversations held under her glow. This is me. Acknowledging the hurt and the nastiness in hopes that it will lose its hold over me. In doing so I hope I can make someone out there feel less insane, less alone, and above all else seen.

Acknowledgements

I would like to take a moment to thank myself. Opening myself and my story to the world like this is crazy and not anything I planned on ever doing. I told no one about this little passion project and somehow remained some what on track. I see you doing your thing and finding the light.

1. Sardines

Full bed
Five of us
Lined up like sardines

A knee to the back
An arm in my face
And the endless snores
That kept me up

Nine people
Stuffed inside a tiny
One bedroom apartment

An eight hour drive
Took me from
Everything I had ever known

No goodbyes

So angry

So hurt
So confused

Still
I understood
Why things had to be this way
I understood what it all meant

I saw the sadness
In your tired eyes

Only now
I realize
Just how tired they really were
A lifetime of heart ache
Held inside such a small frame

Let down so many times
By so many people

How did you continue mama
Cause I am drowning
Plagued by all the things
You once faced

And I fear

That I do not carry
Your strength

2. Breath

I am drowning
I can feel the water
Slowly filing my lungs

I close my eyes and try
To take a breath
Hoping for the crisp air
To hit my lungs

But
I am met
With more water

I open my eyes
Push it to the side
Maybe I will face it all tomorrow...

I have learned to live

With lungs
Carrying oceans within

3. Moon

The moon
In her light you embraced me
Healed my trust
Whispered sweet nothings

Wrapped in a blanket cocoon
Laughing under the stars

The moon
Once a reminder
Of that night
Painted anew with laughter

The moon and the stars
The only witnesses to
Our beautiful experience

You gave me such peace
And when I see the moon
I can still see your smile

Illuminated by the sky light

The moon
I hope you see her beauty
And think of me too

Our time has passed but when I look up to the sky
I still feel your hand holding mine
Wrapped in a world of our own

4. Naive

He said it wasn't an insult

Yet
Naive

This one word
Wiped out every lesson learned

I learned many

My heart
Carries these scars

Naive
How could one word
Invalidate everything

Experience

I do not lack

I simply refuse

This world and the people in it
I won't let them
Change me

Not again

No I am not naive
I know all too well

The monsters
Too many hide
Within their flesh and bones

I am all too familiar with them

The hurt their lies bring
No I am not naive

Though a fool
Perhaps once
Or twice

5. Five

The tv on
The five of us around a coffee table enjoying our meal
Mom couldn't afford a table yet
But this is the most at home I'd ever feel
The five of us laughing til our bellies hurt
Mom waiting til we had our fill to eat
I was always aware of how hard times were
But when it was the five of us
They never felt so bad
Of course it was hard
But distance has erased those moments
And I can only remember the laughter
The love
The peace
The innocence
I think I'll spend my whole life
Reminiscing on these times
Wishing I could laugh like that once more
But we grew
And slowly we all left home

There's no more laughter that makes my belly hurt
There's no one to annoy
There's no more meals on the floor around a coffee table
There's no more clashing personalities
No more movie nights
No more puzzles
But my heart is so full of theses memories
They flood my head
When it gets dark
And they remind me that love is real
For it was there
That I felt it the most
Sitting around that coffee table
The tv on

Still
I Find myself turning it on
Constantly
Hoping the sound will fill the silence
And take me back
To when things didn't feel so dark

6. Sun Beams

You felt
Like sun beams
Warming my skin

Your presence lingering
Floating like specs of dust
Illuminated by
Sun Beams

When you touched my heart
You touched it gently
So cautiously

You tainted
Not a single memory
We had our time

We said our goodbyes
Silently
But your warmth remains

7. Life preserver

You were his life preserver
The floating debris
The aftermath of a wreckage

You were simply
Where he laid his head to rest
When there was no where else

His life line
When he had nothing else
He held onto you so tightly

You felt his empty embrace
You met only his surface
You thought it was love
You thought it was real

But the rescue team came
And he left you
And you knew

You were nothing but floating debris
Something to keep him from going under

Yes something
Not someone

He never saw *you*
Only what you could do for him

Nothing but a last resort

I know

A broken man once laid his head on me too

8. Melancholy

I was born with a deep melancholy inside of me
I've felt it my whole life
Always lingering at the back ground of every happy
moment
Waiting to carry away any happiness
Wondering how long the joy would last
When would it be ripped away from me
Because I always knew
This too
Would come to an end
Nothing good ever seemed to stay

Yes I was born melancholy
Grieving a lost uncle
Grieving a father that would never be mine
I felt this melancholy at 5
And again at 8
And all the time between

I see now

I was robbed
I was a thief
Robbing myself of any chance of happiness
Refusing to let in the light
Without fear
Always grieving what could have been
And what once was

9. Golden dream

I wish to find joy
Although most days it seems to flee
My mind is set to destroy

The days I do find it seem like a decoy
A trap set to let the destruction run free
I wish to find joy

I want to frolic and enjoy
To be so full of glee
My mind is set to destroy

Happiness, I wish to enjoy
A golden dream that will never be
I wish to find joy

But these shadows lurk waiting to destroy
How I wish it was just me
My mind is set to destroy

I feel a glimmer but it is a ploy
Still I'll fight for love and cheer
I wish to find joy
My mind is set to destroy

10. The consequences of my own actions

Well well well if it isn't the consequences of my own
actions
Caught up to me like a train at full speed
I say I have bad luck
But that's not it, is it?

No no no it's the consequences of my own actions
They came barreling at me like a tidal wave
I ignored the voice inside my head
The feeling in my gut
And this is a score I must settle

Yes yes yes it's the consequences of my own actions
Charging at me like a bull seeing red
I can't be angry anymore
I knew the price
And still I wagered

Do not pay me any attention
While I pay the price

11. Back to me

Before him I moved mountains
My voice it swayed the trees
But he wanted me small
So I shrunk myself
Stripped myself of everything
That made me, me
My dreams were put on a shelf

So please be patient
As I fall in love with life
As I fix my damaged parts
As I find my way
Back to me

12. Ships

I had this fire
Burning inside me

Watching the world around me
Carry on
Running towards their dreams

There I stood
Anchored

A pinnacle
Watching the ships
Sail off into the sun

13. Fight or flight

Fight or Flight
Adrenaline kicks in
Heart rate speeds up
And the pain numbs

It is in these moments
You see the savage within

The instinct
To fight or flight

I know the pain inflicted
Was a simple instinct

So why do I sit here
With this weight inside me

This guilt

I feel a debt

I must pay

So why are you
So carefree?

14. Spiral

This exhaustion
I feel it in my bones
Somewhere deep within

It's 10pm
I should be asleep
I look over
You've been asleep since 9

It's 11pm
I still can't sleep
I look over
What did you mean
when you said
sssss

It's 12am
I'm not even tired
I look over
How could some one so close

Feel so far

It's 1am
I wish I could go for a run
I look over
All the woman rush to my mind

It's 2am
I really wish I could sleep
I look over
Are we here only out of obligation?

It's 3am
I really can't sleep
I look over
I see you
I think of when we first met
19 with your cartoon Christmas sweater
Courteous
Shy
Gentle

It's 4am
I've given up on sleep
I look over
Your eyes are open
You ask for a back rub

I wish I could see myself through your eyes
Where did it go wrong?
Is it us?
Is it you?
Is it me?
Are just not meant to be?
Why is it this hard?
It shouldn't be this hard
I should be able to sleep

It's 5 am
I feel a little tired now
I look over
The man that I love

It's 6am
My eyes are heavy
I look over
And fall asleep

15. Worst Part

The worst part
Wasn't the ringing in my ear
The worst part
Wasn't the taste of blood in my mouth
The worst part
Wasn't watching you cry after
The worst part
Wasn't that for my first mothers day my only gift was a
bruised face
The worst part
Wasn't having my parents ask how it happened
Nor was it the sad look in their eyes
Telling me
We know

No the worst part
Is that the next time it happened
I was ready

16. The moon through the window

The moon through the window
For so long
That was all I remembered

She was tucked away
Hidden within the trees
Scared

Looking on
Unable to help
Unable to move

The memories trickled in
Slowly

And then
A flash
And my heart sinks
My insides free falling

I do not want to remember
I do not want to remember

17. Life Line

You were born after me

But for as long as I can remember
You were the big one
I was too afraid to talk
So you'd talk for me

You were born after me

But when I was called weird
You would defend me

You were born after me

But when he left me
One phone call
You dropped everything
And came to rescue me

You were born after me

But you've always been the big one

18. Love

I only see the bad in him
Is what he said
That I never appreciate
The effort

But if you ask my friend
She would tell you
I forgave too many times

If you ask my sisters
They would tell you
I cried too many tears

If you ask my brothers
They would tell you
Of the times they picked me up

If you ask my parents
They would tell you
That I tried too hard

For too long

But
If you were to ask me
I would tell you

That it was love
That it never left
That maybe we're just too different

I would speak of his ambition
With a sparkle in my eyes

I would tell you
That his chest
Was my home

That I do not believe
He wanted to hurt me

That I hope he knows
I never wanted to hurt him

But we did
And there is no way back

We walked across
And burned the bridge

35

19. Same Blood

Our blood is not the same
But when the truth is heavy
And the world makes no sense
I think of you

I think of old pictures
Of you and I
You had no obligation
To love or care for me
But you did

You fed me
You bathed me
You hugged me
You clothed me
Most importantly
You were there

I think of you and I remember
Our blood is not the same

It tears at me

I had this voice
For too long
It told me
No matter what I did
What I said

Our blood was not the same
I did not carry your name
That even if you did love me
It was not the same

That you would never care for me
The way you did for my brothers

This voice
The older I became
The louder it became
The more it echoed

We started to drift
I could feel it
I made daggers of my words
I spoke of our blood
Out of anger
Out of sadness

I got older
They told me
That our bond is not the same
Because our blood is not the same

But it is your voice
Inside of my head
Telling me that I must carry on

That life is not fair
That I can choose
To be
Or not
But I must never choose to stay stuck
Crippled by the anger of every injustice

It is your
Know it all attitude
That I carry

It is because of you
That I cannot
Sit idly by
When someone is in need

And when you are hurt

Even if you pretend
That you do not care
I know that you do
It is this
Brush it off mentality
That I carry

Now it doesn't hurt to say
Our blood is not the same
Because you and I never cared much about that
Anyway
Let the rest fade

Because you chose me
And I chose you

You love me
I love you

Thank you for being
My father
Thank you for being
You

20. Blood

Your betrayal hurt
More
Than his
We carry the same blood
But you never asked for my side of the story
Because you never cared

Instead every memory we had
Was tainted

I refuse to brush it off
I was told to let go
The way we do
Everything else
No conversation needed
No resolution
No understanding

Because you couldn't be bothered
To ask

For my side of the story

The hurt wouldn't leave
And my baby girl was born

She carries this sadness
This sensitivity

And I wonder
If all the tears
I shed
Reached her
And I'm filled
With this rage
All over again

His betrayal
And yours
Come back
Like an electric shock
Everywhere
All at once

Brought on by a child's tears

I kept it in
I let it fester

And it consumed me

It felt never ending
Most days
Until I sat

And realized
The void had consumed me
Left only with the outline
Of who I once was

So this is me
Letting go
Of both of you
The hurt
The anger
Everything

21. New villain

I used to fear
Being the villain in your story
Now I would gladly take the role

In hopes
You will not reach for my hand
Once more

If I cannot reach for yours
I will gladly be the villain
And watch you slowly fade
Into the dark blue abyss